Diary of a SNOWBOARDING Freak

www.heinemann.co.uk/library

Visit our website to find out more information about **Heinemann Library** books.

To order:
☎ Phone 44 (0) 1865 888066
🖹 Send a fax to 44 (0) 1865 314091
💻 Visit the Heinemann Bookshop at www.heinemann.co.uk/library to browse our catalogue and order online.

Produced by Monkey Puzzle Media Ltd
Gissing's Farm, Fressingfield, Suffolk IP21 5SH, UK

First published in Great Britain by Heinemann Library, Halley Court, Jordan Hill, Oxford OX2 8EJ, part of Harcourt Education.
Heinemann is a registered trademark of Harcourt Education Ltd.

Author: Paul Mason
Editorial: Otto De'ath
Series Designer: Tim Mayer
Book Designer: Vicky Short
Illustrator: Sam Lloyd
Production: Séverine Ribierre

Originated by Repro Multi-Warna
Printed in Hong Kong, China by Wing King Tong

ISBN 0 431 17540 3
07 06 05 04 03
10 9 8 7 6 5 4 3 2 1

British Library Cataloguing in Publication Data
Mason, Paul
Diary of a Snowboarding Freak
796.9
A full catalogue record for this book is available from the British Library.

Acknowledgements
With thanks to **Tudor Thomas/White Lines** magazine for supplying all photographs, with the exception of: **front cover** (inset), **back cover**, pp. **3** (all but top right), **4–8** (all), **9** (all but bottom right), **11** (bottom right), **14–15** (all), **16–17** (bottom sequence), **22** (all), **24–25** (all), **26** (bottom), **27** (bottom left) supplied by **Mike Weyerhaeuser/JDP Photography**.

Every effort has been made to contact copyright holders of any material reproduced in this book. Any omissions will be rectified in subsequent printings if notice is given to the publishers.

Attention!
This book is about snowboarding, which is a dangerous sport. The book is not a substitute for proper lessons. Readers are advised to get lessons from a qualified instructor, always wear the appropriate safety equipment and never ride the mountain alone.

CONTENTS

Snowboarding words are explained in the glossary on page 30.

I AM A SNOWBOARDING FREAK

Kylie Buchanan Fact File:
Age: Sixteen
Years riding: Three
Favourite food: Steck frites fromage (a baguette with hot steak, chips, cheese and thousand-island sauce) from Poco Loco in Chamonix.
Hobbies: Snowboarding (obviously), surfing and knitting. But I'm lying about the knitting.

This is me!

I'm writing this sitting in a cramped room in a snowboard lodge in the mountains. The smelly snowboard boots, wet pants and jackets, and the three people sharing the room have made a smell I've never smelt before. The window's open to let in some fresh air.

It snowed last night. In a minute we're catching the first lift up the mountain to do a run we've been looking at for a while. It hasn't had enough snow for over a month, since the snowboarding camp started. I think today we'll finally polish it off. But for now I'm scribbling a few lines to introduce my diary: the diary of the last two years, and how I got into snowboarding. The diary of a snowboard freak.

Me plus kit at home, before we came out here.

Taken last week! Me and Jenna near one of the little drag lifts halfway up the mountain. I don't know why we're looking so happy: we both hate drag lifts and we were just about to have to do one!

Jenna took this of me last winter, on a good, sunny powder day.

5

DECEMBER

2	9	16	23	30
3	10	17	24	31
4	11	18	25	
5	12	19	26	
6	13	20	27	
7	14	21	28	
1	8	15	22	29

Lifts! I really hate lifts; they're all designed for skiers, who face forwards not sideways.

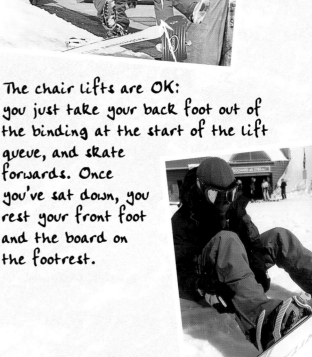

SATURDAY 28 DECEMBER
THE EARLY YEARS

Oww! I had no idea when I heard we were coming skiing for the first time that it would hurt like this. Dad says it's because I chose to go my own way and snowboard instead. He might be right, but I think snowboarding's a lot more cool, even if you do pick up a few bruises.

We've been here for five days, and I've caught the snowboarding bug (even though my bum hurts like never before). I'm going to keep a diary of my career as a snowboarder: I think I'm going to be coming again, because we've all really enjoyed it here.

The chair lifts are OK: you just take your back foot out of the binding at the start of the lift queue, and skate forwards. Once you've sat down, you rest your front foot and the board on the footrest.

6

Drag lifts are really tricky as Dad's photo of me falling over shows!

Jenna's first proper turn, captured on film by me!

Snowboard language:

Backside: A turn on the heel-edge side of the board.

Binding: The thing that attaches your boots to the board.

Fakie: Riding backwards.

Frontside: A turn on the toe-edge side of the board.

Goofy foot: Someone who rides with their right foot forwards.

Regular foot: Someone who rides with their left foot forwards.

1) GOING DOWNHILL STARTING A BACKSIDE TURN.

2) SHE SORT OF SAT DOWN A BIT: BENT HER KNEES AND HIPS, SO THAT THE WEIGHT WENT ON HER HEELS AND THE HEEL EDGE OF THE BOARD. SHE SAID THE MOVEMENT WAS EASIER IF SHE LIFTED HER HANDS UP TOWARDS HER SHOULDERS.

3) NEXT SHE SHOULD HAVE EASED OFF THE TURN BY STANDING UP FROM THE SITTING POSITION AND PULLING HER HANDS DOWN TOWARDS HER HIPS. THEN SHE COULD HAVE CARRIED ON TO TURN THE OTHER WAY. UNFORTUNATELY JENNA WAS GOING TOO FAST, SO SHE JUST CARRIED ON WITH THE TURN UNTIL SHE STOPPED!

NOTE TO SELF:

KEEP STANCE NEUTRAL!

Apparently beginners often lean back, over the tail of the board. It's best to keep your weight spread between both feet.

MARCH

	10	17	24	31
	11	18	25	
	12	19	26	
	13	20	27	
	14	21	28	
1	15	22	29	
2	16	23	30	

3
4
5
6
7
8
9

MONDAY 17 MARCH
SPRINGTIME, SECOND GO

Springtime in the Alps, and what's even better is that we're back here so soon! Even better than THAT, there's a really good group of people my age out here, and Jenna and I have been out boarding with them.

There's been fresh snow since last time we were here, so the others said we should go out to do some runs in the deep powder beside the pistes. The pistes are the prepared runs laid out around the resort. Leaving these and riding in the unprepared areas between the pistes gets you into deeper, unprepared snow.

Snowboarders all seem really friendly to each other: we met these guys two days ago, and they've already given us loads of advice.

This is a girl called Becky, catching the nose of her board in the snow and wiping out.

This photo of Dan shows how you should ride in deep powder. His weight is on his back foot, and he's pulling the nose up slightly with his front foot to stop it from burying itself.

Jenna did some good turns, too!

If only I could buy my own board!

Things went badly wrong for this rider, who we saw from the lift.

APRIL

	7	14	21	28
1	8	15	22	29
2	9	16	23	30
3	10	17	24	
4	11	18	25	
5	12	19	26	
6	13	20	27	

Big choice of boards!

All-round boards like this are directional, which means the 'waist' (the narrowest bit) is towards the back of the board.

WEDNESDAY 23 APRIL
BOARD-TASTIC!

Why am I making an entry in my snowboarding diary at the end of April? Because I just got my own gear for the first time, that's why! No more going to the hire shop on my first day in the resort and wasting a whole morning. Next winter I'll be fully prepared and ready for the first lift on the first day.

There were a lot of things to think about: there's so much kit out there that I didn't really know what to get. But the guy in the shop was a snowboarder himself, and he was really helpful. It was even all reduced in the end-of-winter sale!

This is a specialist powder board. I like riding powder, but I need to be able to get round the whole mountain on the pistes as well. That swallow tail might not be great for that.

This board is designed specially for women. A few manufacturers make these, but this one's for advanced riders.

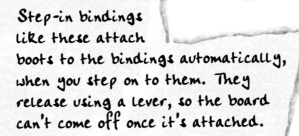

Step-in bindings like these attach boots to the bindings automatically, when you step on to them. They release using a lever, so the board can't come off once it's attached.

These are strap bindings with boots designed to go with them. You have to sit down in the snow to do them up, but lots of riders prefer the way they feel.

Couldn't wait to put the whole lot together once I'd bought it!

APRIL

	7	14	21	28
1	8	15	22	29
2	9	16	23	30
3	10	17	24	
4	11	18	25	
5	12	19	26	
6	13	20	27	

SATURDAY 26 APRIL
I'M A CLOTHES HORSE!

Raining all day today — can't go out skateboarding (good practice for snowboarding). Prices in the sale at the snowboard shop were really low. I've done a bit of research into maybe getting some new clothes (watch out, watch out, savings account!).

Last winter I definitely felt like I wanted some better trousers. The ones I borrowed didn't fit over snowboard boots that well, and soaked through when I sat in the snow to do my bindings up. I'd like to get some really warm stuff: I remember it being ever so hard to learn new techniques once I was cold.

HOOD FOR SNOWY AND COLD DAYS.

FULL-LENGTH ZIP WITH COVER TO KEEP OUT WIND.

MAP/SUNGLASSES/ GOGGLES/CD PLAYER POCKET.

POCKET FOR LIFT PASS.

SNOW SKIRT KEEPS OUT SNOW WHEN YOU FALL OVER. THIS WOULD MAKE EVERYTHING MUCH MORE COMFORTABLE!

CUFFS THAT CAN BE TIGHTENED OVER OR UNDER GLOVES.

Handy toolkit

OTHER STUFF I'D GET IF
I WERE SUPER-RICH:

- New backpack.

- New fleece and thermals.

- Tool kit.

- Wristguards, helmet and
padded motocross-style shorts
for protection.

- New gloves with removable
inners, which dry more quickly.

- New goggles.

So that's new everything, really...

Backpack
for extra
kit

Goggles

ELASTICATED WAIST
AT THE BACK FOR
FLEXIBILITY.

ggle

Warm gloves

INNER GAITERS
TO STOP
SNOW GOING
UP YOUR LEG.

KNEES
ARTICULATED
(BENT) TO
STOP THEM
RUBBING AT
THE BACK.

Wicked helmet!

13

DECEMBER

1	8	15	22	29
2	9	16	23	30
3	10	17	24	31
4	11	18	25	
5	12	19	26	
6	13	20	27	
7	14	21	28	

We can string together turns on almost any slope now. Last year I had to pick a spot to turn really carefully. Now I usually just turn when I feel like it.

SATURDAY 20 DECEMBER

BACKSIDE TO FRONTSIDE

At last, back in the Alps! Best of all, I'm staying with Jenna and Cathy at Cathy's family's chalet, and we're here for the whole Christmas break. I wish I could live here all winter or all year! We met up with a lot of the same people as last year: some of them are out here staying at a training camp for the whole winter!

It was great to try my board out on real snow. All that practice at the indoor snowdome has paid off, too. We're a lot better than when we headed home last year. For proof, I just looked back to compare the sequence of my turns with the one of Jenna when we were learning, on page 7!

THE BACKSIDE TECHNIQUE IS THE SAME AS WHEN WE WERE LEARNING. I'M JUST BETTER AT IT NOW!

JUST FOR A MOMENT THE BOARD GOES FLAT, BUT YOU DON'T REALLY NOTICE IT BECAUSE YOUR BODY'S ALREADY INTO THE TURN. INSTEAD OF SITTING YOUR WEIGHT INTO YOUR HEELS, YOU DROP YOUR WEIGHT ONTO YOUR SHINS. THE TOE EDGE OF THE BOARD STARTS TO BITE.

SOME PEOPLE BEND THEIR BACK KNEE IN MORE THAN OTHERS TO PUSH THE BOARD ROUND. OTHER PEOPLE TURN THEIR BODY TO THE FRONT LESS THAN I DO, TOO.

JANUARY

5	12	19	26
6	13	20	27
7	14	21	28
1 8	15	22	29
2 9	16	23	30
3 10	17	24	31
4 11	18	25	

Simon Brass pulling off a massive aerial in the pipe.

THURSDAY 1 JANUARY
JUMP GODDESS

We're going back home soon, and I was determined to manage to do a decent jump before we do. The practice on Friday nights at the snowdome has really helped: they set up little obstacles and picnic tables for people to jump off, and I've done some of those. It meant I knew not to be scared of going towards a jump quite fast – it seems to make the takeoff and landing smoother, unless anything goes wrong.

We went over to the fun park yesterday. Cathy's brother Mike took some groovy shots of me looking like a real pro.

BEND YOUR KNEES AS YOU GO UP THE RAMP, AND LET YOUR SPEED CARRY YOU OFF IT. IT'S TRICKY TO GET YOUR SPEED RIGHT AT FIRST. IT'S IMPORTANT TO GO FAST ENOUGH OR YOU MIGHT NOT EVEN GET OFF THE JUMP!

16

SOME PEOPLE FIND GRABBING
THE SIDE OF THE BOARD HELPS
THEM BALANCE IN THE AIR.

This is Lesley
McKenna!

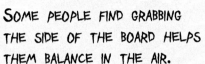

Maybe next year I'll
be good enough to go
into the half-pipe.
At the moment it
looks terrifying,
but I spoke to one
of the other girls
in the fun park
and she said it
was OK. Then I
discovered I'd
been talking to
Lesley McKenna — who's
been in the Olympics!

TRY TO LAND TAIL FIRST
AND BEND YOUR KNEES TO
ABSORB THE LANDING.

17

US POWDER HOUND

Yay! Just got home to find an email from Jake, my stepbrother in America. He lives with my dad's first wife in California. They can snowboard in the morning (at a resort called 'Heavenly'!) and surf in the evening, by driving for a few hours in between.

Inbox Compose Addresses Folders Options Print Help
Reply Reply All Forward Delete Previous Next Close

From: Jake
Date: January 7
To: Kylie
Subject: US Powder Hound

>Hey, Kylie, how's it going?

We've just been up to Lake Tahoe for the weekend: it's a great place, you'd love it. It's not like Europe, where you stay in the resort that you're riding in. Here, you stay further down the mountain and then drive up to whichever resort you want to each day. There are loads of different resorts around Tahoe, but Heavenly's my favourite.

We just had a lot of fresh snow. We took the digital video camera up there and shot loads of sequences. I've sent still shots of me doing a turn to show you what the conditions were like. Also a few still shots of other riders you could print.

>Jake

Brother Jake
making a turn
in some deep
powder.

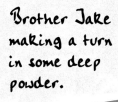

This looks like half
of a natural half-
pipe. A natural
quarter-pipe, then...

Look how deep that powder is!
Some US resorts get 10 metres of
snow in places, apparently.

19

MARCH

1	8	15	22	29
2	9	16	23	30
3	10	17	24	31
4	11	18	25	
5	12	19	26	
6	13	20	27	
7	14	21	28	

This was how we first saw the boardercross course, from one of the big bubble lifts. ➜

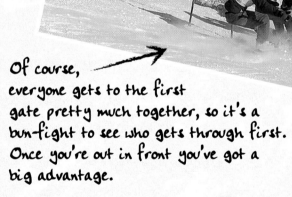

SATURDAY 27 MARCH
BOARDERCROSS BATTLES

Today we stumbled across a boardercross competition. I hadn't heard of this before, and it's absolutely bonkers! A group of riders – usually four of them – set off together down a specially made course. The course has banked turns and jumps, and the idea is to get down it fastest. The quickest rider wins.

It looked fun, but really dangerous. There's lots of pushing, shoving, falling over and crashing. Even snowboarders who don't wear a helmet in the half-pipe wear one in boardercross. And they're not just ordinary helmets – some people seemed to be wearing full-face motocross-style ones!

Of course, ➜ everyone gets to the first gate pretty much together, so it's a bun-fight to see who gets through first. Once you're out in front you've got a big advantage.

20

Wheee!

There was quite a little crowd of spectators waiting to see people crash. They weren't disappointed!

Helmets are required in boardercross events: the only regular snowboard competitions where you always have to wear a helmet.

21

MARCH

1	8	15	22	29
2	9	16	23	30
3	10	17	24	31
4	11	18	25	
5	12	19	26	
6	13	20	27	
7	14	21	28	

We hiked up the slope, then had to have a little lie down to recover. We need to get fitter!

MONDAY 29 MARCH
THE NEXT
HAAKONSEN

We've been watching an old video called *Subjekt: Haakonsen* that someone left in the chalet. It's about one of the all-time great riders, Terje Haakonsen. We've found some old photos of him in a half-pipe competition in the USA, but they don't really show how fluid he was, and the amazing height he got from his jumps.

Terje did it all — half-pipe, off-piste, fun park — and he skated and surfed really well too. Like a lot of top snowboarders, he refused to go to the first Olympics that had snowboarding. He felt it went against the friendly, casual spirit of the sport. I've decided that I need to get fit enough to be like Terje!

Jake sent me a URL for a 'what's hot' list for healthy eating. He reckons they know all about it in California!

TOP TIPS

A balanced diet is the key.
Eat plenty of fruit and vegetables, as well as some fresh, unprocessed meat, fish and cheese.

What's hot:
Fresh fruit, vegetables: steamed is best.
Fresh meat; fresh fish, grilled or barbecued.
Newly baked bread; pasta; cheese.

What's not:
Processed burgers.
Fried food (meat, fish or vegetables).
Too much fatty food: mayonnaise, cheese etc. A little is OK though!
Sweets and chocolate.
Too much sugar in cakes, etc.

Terje Haakonsen.

NOTE TO SELF:

• Always remember to warm up before exercising and snowboarding, and do some stretching afterwards to avoid feeling sore the next day.

• Swimming's easier than running as a way of building up fitness right through my body.

23

JUNE

7	14	21	28
1	8	15	22	29
2	9	16	23	30
3	10	17	24
4	11	18	25
5	12	19	26
6	13	20	27

Some people stayed in motorhomes; most of us camped in tents, on a campsite nearby.

MONDAY 7 JUNE
SUMMER CAMP

My plan to be allowed to go away for the whole of next winter hasn't quite come off – yet. But this is the next-best thing – snowboarding summer camp. The organizers set it up specially for people my age, so there are loads of people I get on with really well.

Down here in the valley it's really hot, and there's no snow anywhere. We ride up to the glacier on the cable car and then a chair lift every morning. We don't get to snowboard for that long: in the morning it's too icy, and later in the afternoon it's too slushy to be much fun. But there's coaching, and the whole camping thing is really good fun, especially in the evening.

It felt really strange at first, riding up in the sunshine and warm air to go snowboarding. Nice to only have to wear a T-shirt, though, and be able to sunbathe!

24

A special piste-making machine cuts out the half-pipe, but we all had to lend a hand building up the jumps!

The evening fireside chatting was really good fun.

You don't usually see these on a snowboarding trip!

25

FEBRUARY

	7	14	21	28
1	8	15	22	
2	9	16	23	
3	10	17	24	
4	11	18	25	
5	12	19	26	
6	13	20	27	

SATURDAY 12 FEBRUARY
FIRST COMPETITION

After all that practice at summer camp, I've decided to enter a half-pipe competition. I went and registered yesterday, and the competition starts tomorrow after lunch. Am feeling very nervous: wonder if I'll sleep tonight?

Looking down the pipe for the first time, I thought it looked massive! But I managed not to fall over, and I got to the bottom without looking stupid. Yay!

SUNDAY 14 FEBRUARY

Just got back. Didn't make a total fool of myself, thank God: that's all I was worried about. After practice, we started by each having a chance to do a run. The judges were looking for the highest, most radical moves, as well as how many each competitor managed in their run. Then 16 of us got to do a second run, and the judges picked the winner. I came 12th!

Taking a break between runs.

26

This is where everyone lined up, ready to drop in.

The trouble with riding all the way down is that you have to walk all the way back up. But you get to see moves like this one right next to where you're walking.

The judges.

HEROES

Trapped indoors by a massive snowstorm. Thank goodness the chalet's got an Internet connection. My Dad brought his laptop computer, so I've been finding out about some of the great snowboarders from the past and present.

The most inspiring of all was Jake Burton Carpenter — the same person as the 'Burton' snowboarding equipment manufacturer! He had the idea of modifying a childhood toy called a Snurfer, and even though at one point in 1979 he was US$100,000 in debt, he stuck with the idea. When snowboarding started to be accepted in ski resorts, it took off. Now Burton goods are sold in over 30 different countries.

JUSSI OKSANEN

Born: 5/9/79, Kirkkonummi, Finland
Lives: Kirkkonummi, Finland
Occupation: Pro snowboarder
Snowboarding since: 1990
Specialism: Aerials
Career highlights: 2000 winner, Big Air US Open, Vermont; 2001 third place, World Snowboarding Championship, Canada

ROMAN DE MARCHI

Born: 11/10/79
Lives: Geneva, Switzerland
Occupation: Pro snowboarder
Snowboarding since: 1991/1992
Specialism: Aerials
Career highlights: 2002 US Open Best Trick, Quarter-pipe; 2001 third place Innsbruck Air & Style Expression Session, Innsbruck, Austria

He may be in his 40s now, but Jake still rips!

28

DANNY WHEELER

Born: 21/10/76
Lives: Bourg St-Maurice, France
Occupation: Pro snowboarder
Snowboarding since: 1991/1992
Specialism: Aerials
Career highlights: 2002 winner,
Big Air competition, Turin, Italy

I wanted to find out about
Lesley, especially as I've met
her and she's been on TV!

Danny's ranked
as the best
British rider at
the moment.

LESLEY McKENNA

Born: 9/8/74
Lives: Aviemore, Scotland
Occupation: Pro snowboarder
Snowboarding since: 1995
Specialism: Half-pipe,
boardercross, slalom
Career highlights: British
Champion 1997–2000; 2001
second, FIS World Cup half-pipe,
Berchtesgaden, Germany; 2001
ranked number 3 in the world

SNOWBOARDING LANGUAGE

Backside
A turn or move made on the heel-edge side of the board.

Binding
The device that attaches ('binds') a snowboard boot to a snowboard.

Boardercross
A competition where a number of riders (usually four) race side-by-side down a kind of snow obstacle course.

Button lift
A kind of lift with a disc of plastic on the end of an extendable pole. The top of the pole is attached to a lift mechanism: boarders place the disc behind their thighs with the pole between their legs and are dragged along.

Chair lift
A lift you can sit on, which picks skiers and boarders up and carries them to the top of the slope.

Drag lift
A lift that drags boarders and skiers up the mountainside. The main kinds are button lifts and T-bar lifts.

Frontside
A turn or move made on the toe-edge side of the board.

Fun park
An area with specially made obstacles, jumps, etc. for snowboarders to use.

Goofy foot
Someone who rides with their right foot to the front.

Half-pipe
A specially made steep-sided chute: riders zig-zag back and forth, doing jumps off the steep sides.

Kicker
A small jump.

Piste
A marked run, which has usually been prepared for use by the resort management. Obstacles like tree stumps and rocks are cleared away and the snow is compacted down.

Powder
Light, fluffy snow that has not been compacted down.

Quarter-pipe
Imagine half of a half-pipe (a one-sided half-pipe) — that's what a quarter-pipe looks like.

Regular foot
Someone who rides with their left foot in front.

Run
A route down the mountain.

Step-in binding
A binding that allows the rider to step on to the board and ride away, because it attaches automatically under the rider's weight.

Strap binding
A binding that uses straps to attach the boot to the board, and has to be done up by hand.

Summer camp
A summertime snowboard trip, where people camp on the warm valley floor but travel up to a glacier each day to go snowboarding.

INTERNET LINKS

www.uksnowboard.co.uk
This is the on-line home of the British Snowboarding Federation.

www.boarderzone.com
An on-line magazine for news about the international snowboard scene.

www.snowboardaustralia.org.au

BOOKS AND MAGAZINES

The World Snowboard Guide
(Ice Publishing, first edition 1996 but updated every year) has information about many of the world's snowboarding resorts.

To The Limit: Snowboarding by Paul Mason (Hodder Wayland, 2000) has lots of info on all aspects of snowboarding, in an easy-to-read format.

Radical Sports: Snowboarding by Andy Fraser (Heinemann Library, 2000) has essential information on skills and techniques.

White Lines is the best UK snowboarding magazine.

Snowboard UK is also interesting. Like White Lines, it carries interviews with stars, travel articles, examples of technique and news about the sport.

INDEX